How To Control Your Emotions

Excerpts From *Overcoming Bad Habits*

LOY B. SWEEZY, JR.

Copyright © 2008 by Loy B. Sweezy, Jr
How To Control Your Emotions
Published by Loy Sweezy Ministries
    P.O. Box 131
    Austell, GA, 30168

Printed in the United States of America

ISBN-10: 0-9717546-7-6
ISBN-13: 978-0-9717546-7-6

Unless otherwise identified, scripture quotations are from the *King James Version of the Bible.* Copyright © 1989 by Thomas Nelson, Inc. All rights reserved.

Scripture quotations marked AMP are from *The Amplified Bible.* Copyright © 1958, 1965, 1987 by the Zondervan Corporation and The Lockman Foundation. Used by permission of Zondervan Bible Publishers. All rights reserved.

Scriptures marked as *"(CEV)"* are taken from the Contemporary English Version Copyright © 1995 by American Bible Society. Used by Permission.

www.loysweezy. com

Table of Contents

Chapter 1

Understanding Emotions

When I was attending East Coast Bible College, located in Charlotte, North Carolina, I was one of the players on the basketball team. During the away games I noticed that when our team would shoot free throws, especially when the games were really close, the fans behind the basketball goal would wave their hands back and forth; some would use pom-poms; they made all kinds of weird noises and looks with their faces in attempts to distract us and cause us to miss the free throws.

When walking up to the free throw line to shoot the free throws, I noticed that the fans would be calling our names and jersey numbers. If we would focus in on what we heard or looked at the distracting fans we would miss the free throw(s) every single time.

This is the same outcome that your negative emotions will have on you if they go unchecked. You will continue to shoot or aim at your desires but miss; you will lose sight of what you were focused on. Negative emotions will always carry you away from your purpose; they will cause you to lose out. Also, negative emotions can have a bad affect on all those who are associated or are a part of what you are doing.

Your emotions are a vital part of your life. Your emotions never sleep; even in dreams your emotions will still respond a certain way to what you are dreaming about. There are good emotions and there are bad emotions.

Good emotions are designed to produce life and peace within your life, while bad or negative emotions are designed to pull you away from God and the things of God, ultimately, producing destruction in your life.

Controlling your emotions starts with one thing—you making the decision that it is possible to control your emotions. *"Jesus said unto him, If thou canst believe, all things are possible to him that believeth" (Mark 9:23).* You can manage your emotions; one of the keys to managing your emotions is to know that it is possible to control them.

The Bible states that God gave Adam and Eve dominion (Genesis 1:26, 28); the word **dominion** means *supreme authority or control.* The word dominion carries with it the connation of having the ability or the legal right to rule and to exercise. So then what is it that God has given to the Body of Christ? It is the right to rule and have supreme authority over their emotions.

What is an emotion? According to the American Heritage Dictionary, an **emotion** is defined as *the part of the consciousness that involves feelings and sensibility.* Emotions are energized feelings; when emotions come on you, the feelings will flow throughout your body. An emotion, clinically speaking, has to do with an intense feeling or a strong desire for something whether or not it is right or wrong.

Emotions will begin in the mind (consciousness) which is psychological, and then they will move you into a reaction caused by feelings of expression, which is physiological. If your emotions do not line up with the Word of God, or if they go against the Word of God, then the emotions you are feeling are not from God (Philippians 4:4-8).

It is important to understand that if you are born of God (Christian) you can overcome your negative emotion. *"For whatsoever is born of God overcometh the world: and this is the victory that overcometh the world, even our faith (I John 5:4).* You were created by God to win. With God on your side you don't win some of the time, you win all the time.

You do not have to be carried away and driven by your negative circumstances and situations. Again, God has placed within every born again believer (Christian) the ability to win. The Bible states, *"Nay, in all these things we are more than conquerors through him that loved us" (Romans 8:37).* You can win over your negative emotions; you can control how you will respond to things that you hear, see and feel.

Another important thing to understand about your emotions is that YOU are the responsible party for determining how you will respond to what you feel, see, think and hear.

Notice this scripture,

> *"I call heaven and earth to record this day against you, that I have set before you life and death, blessing and cursing: therefore choose life, that both thou and thy seed may live. (Deuteronomy 30:19)*

God has given you the ability to succeed. However, you are going to be responsible for choosing and acting on your authority as a believer to receive the manifestation in the area that you desire.

Jesus said, *"Behold, I give unto you power to tread on serpents and scorpions, and over all the power of*

the enemy: and nothing shall by any means hurt you"
(Luke 10:19). Although Jesus has given you power
over all the enemy, which includes your negative
emotions, if you do not choose to take authority over
your emotions then your negative emotions will take
authority over you.

If you do not take control of your negative emotions then your negative emotions will carry you in
the wrong direction. What happens when you go
in the wrong direction? You get farther and farther
away from your destination. Negative emotions will
get you into places that God did not intend for you
to be. You can spend several years recovering from
a bad decision that you made under the influence of
your wrong emotions.

> *"And the Lord said to Cain, Why are you*
> *angry? And why do you look sad and*
> *depressed and dejected? If you do well, will*
> *you not be accepted? And if you do not do*
> *well, sin crouches at your door; its desire is*
> *for you, but you must master it." (Genesis*
> *4:6-7, AMP)*

One of the keys in this verse is the word it. What
is it that God wanted Cain to master? It would be
his uncontrolled emotions (anger and envy) leading
him eventually in a direction that would take him

out of the will of God for his life. God told Cain that you must master it because if he did not master his uncontrolled emotions, they would cause him to do something insane, and then later on he would regret his decision.

You must master your emotions or your emotions will master you. The word **master** means *to control or have authority over.* In Genesis 4:6-7, again, God was communicating to Cain that he had the ability to control his negative emotions. You can control your emotions. You may not be able to control people but you can control how you will respond to people.

Scriptures on Self Control

1.) He that is slow to anger is better than the mighty; and he that **ruleth** his spirit than he that taketh a city. (Proverbs 16:32)

2.) And the spirits of the prophets are **subject** to the prophets. (I Corinthians 14:32)

3.) For the love of Christ **constraineth** us... (II Corinthians 5:14)

4.) But the fruit of the Spirit is love, joy, peace, longsuffering, gentleness, goodness, faith, meekness, **temperance;** against such there is no law. (Galatians 5:22-23)

When a person does not know how to control their emotions they are more prone to lose their temper, get into fights, steal, become easily distracted, engage in prostitution, lesbianism, and homosexuality, and participate in alcohol and drug abuse, lies and so on.

People who <u>do not</u> know how to manage their emotions tend to display these types of behaviors:

- Poor decision making

- Suicidal Ideations

- Low self-esteem

- Sexual perversion

- Extreme boredom

- Chronic agitation

- Severe mood swings

- Uncontrolled substance abuse

- Anger is out of control

- Frequent termination from jobs

People who know how to manage their emotions appropriately tend to display these types of behaviors:

- Make sound judgment and decision making
- Demonstrate serenity/calmness under pressured situations
- Confident in who they are
- Extremely slow to become angry
- Less likely to be terminated from a job
- Open to differences of others to make them better
- Tend to be more happier and enjoy life
- Is not easily offended
- Express emotions appropriately

Chapter 2

Amnon's Uncontrolled Emotions

A good example of negative emotions can be located in (II Samuel 13:1-5, 12, 14, 18, 23, and 32.) I strongly recommend that you read this Chapter in its entirety to grasp its full meaning of what I am communicating.

> "And it came to pass after this, that Absalom the son of David had a fair sister, whose name was Tamar; and Amnon the son of David loved her. And Amnon was so vexed, that he fell sick for his sister Tamar; for she was a virgin; and Amnon thought it hard for him to do anything to her. But Amnon had a friend, whose name was Jonadab, the son of Shimeah David's brother: and Jonabab was a very subtle man. He said unto him, why art thou, being the king's

son lean from day to day? Wilt thou not tell me? Amnon said unto him, I love Tamar, my brother Absalom's sister. And Jonadab said unto him... And she answered him, Nay my brother, do not force me; for no such thing ought to be done in Israel: do not thou this folly... Howbeit he would not hearken unto her voice; but being stronger than she, forced her, and lay with her. Then Amnon hated her exceedingly; so that the hatred wherewith he hated her was greater than the love wherewith he had loved her. And Amnon said unto her, Arise, be gone... Then his servant brought her out, and bolted the door after her... And it came to pass after two years, that Absalom had sheepshears in Baal-hazor, which is beside Ephraim: and Absalom invited all the king's sons... and Jonadab, the son of Shimeah David's brother, answered and said, Let not my lord suppose that they have slain all the young men the king's sons; for Amnon only is dead: for by the appointment of Absalom this hath been determined from the day that he forced his sister Tamar."

First, Amnon's love was lust. Amnon's love for Tamar was built on an emotional fatal attraction and not a genuine commitment. This was displayed when he received what he wanted (sexual relations) by forcing her, and then afterwards, began to hate her. Love does not hate nor will it hurt. Love always desires the best for another person and love will never think of doing evil (I Corinthians 13:4-8). Therefore, the question to be asked is what made Amnon hate Tamar? It was his uncontrolled emotions; his spirit of lust overpowered him causing Tamar shame, and Amnon, eventually, death.

Uncontrolled emotions will always get you into situations that you did not intend to get into. Amnon had no idea that Absalom would eventually kill him over his sister. I am sure Amnon had no idea that he would violate Tamar sexually. That is the trick of uncontrolled emotions; they will set you up to have short pleasure, but after the thrill is gone the devastation of the consequences that follow are never pleasant. The death of Amnon could have been avoided if Amnon would have controlled his negative emotions.

Second, Amnon listened to wrong advice. *"Blessed is the man that walketh not in the counsel of the ungodly" (Psalms 1:1.)* The Amplified states; *BLESSED (Happy,* *fortunate, prosperous, and enviable) is the man who walks and lives not in the counsel of the ungodly [following their advice, their plans and purposes].*

What Ammon's friend (Jonadab) told him to do was very ungodly. Therefore, by Amnon acting on his friend's wrong advice, it cost him his life. Who are you listening too? What they say to you could be a matter of life and death.

In the Garden of Eden (Genesis 3:1-11), Adam and Eve had sinned and discovered that they were naked. Immediately God asked the question, who told you? God knew that they had listened to the wrong advice thus this wrong advice caused separation between them and God. This wrong advice resulted in Jesus Christ dying for humanity to reestablish a spiritual connection between God and man (I Timothy 2:5-6).

Third, your uncontrolled emotions will affect others around you. Whether or not you are aware of your uncontrolled emotions, they will affect the people in your life. Amnon's decision to violate his half sister made his extended family angry with him. Absalom, who is Amnon's brother, was affected by Amnon's decision so badly until he ordered Amnon killed, and at the time that Amnon thought everything was calm and forgotten.

On the other hand, the Bible says (Genesis 41:1,

9) that the butler remembered Joseph's interpretation of his dream two years later because Joseph had a positive, life-lasting affect on him. Joseph and the butler were in prison together; Joseph did something for the butler that he would never forget. Joseph showed the butler kindness by interpreting his dream and showing him comfort until the king released the butler.

When the butler was released from prison and the king needed his dream interpreted, immediately the butler remembered Joseph. This is how Joseph came out of prison; he made a mark, a positive effect that would be life-lasting for the butler to remember.

Amnon's bad decision was remembered two years after he sexually abused his sister and was killed for it, however, Joseph was remembered two years later because of what he did for the butler. Joseph was rewarded by being released from prison and promoted to the second highest position in Egypt—the governor (Genesis 42:6).

You will definitely be remembered for something. Both Joseph and Amnon were remembered for their actions; one was remembered for his good action and the other was remembered for his bad action. What will you be remembered for?

It is also important to indicate that emotions have to do with you making the right or wrong decisions under the influence of intense feelings of pressure applied to the mind. When I say intense feelings of pressure applied to the mind, I am conveying that you will feel emotions, such as fear, anger, guilt or intimidation and will have to work hard and be consistent at doing the right thing, even though your emotions are telling you to do the wrong thing.

Fourth, your uncontrolled emotions will have consequences. We see that because of what Amnon did, his uncontrolled emotion cost him his life, which means that you will have to give an account for what you do. You cannot do wrong and get away with it.

The Bible says,

> *"Don't be misled. Remember that you can't ignore God and get away with it. You will always reap what you sow! Those who live only to satisfy their own sinful desires will harvest the consequences of decay and death. But those who live to please the Spirit will harvest everlasting life from the Spirit, so don't get tired of doing what is good. Don't get discouraged and give up, for we will reap a harvest of blessing at the appropriate time." (Galatians 6:7-9, NLT)*

As a Christian, if you are doing wrong and think that you can continue to do wrong and can get away with it, that is criminal thinking. Your actions always have consequences; this is why you want to develop good habits. Good habits produce good consequences and good consequences are always the results of a good decision that was made.

Chapter 3

Look to God

"*In the beginning God created the heavens and the earth.*" *(Genesis 1:1)*

It is only in God that you will find your true identity and reason for existing. Everything that you do must have its starting point with God. It is God who will give you the creative ability to produce great results; it is God who will give you the knowledge and ability to overcome negative emotions.

> "*Wherefore, seeing we also are compassed about with so great a cloud of witnesses, let us lay aside every weight, and the sin which doth so easily beset us, and let us run with patience the race that is set before us. Looking unto Jesus the author and finisher of our faith; who for the joy that was set before him endured the cross, despising the*

*shame, and is set down at the right hand
of the throne of God." (Hebrews 12:1-2)*

There are two things that can to be noted about
the word **look**. First, the word **look** means *to take
a deep fearless searching inventory inside of oneself,*
to be honest with what you see and to be determined to change by working on what needs to be
better.

Second, the word **look** is used to refer to *literally taking a hold of the Word of God, opening it and
reading it* to understand who God is and what He
(God) has said concerning you and your situation.
Exploring through the pages of the Bible with this
thought in mind, whatever is wrong in my life God
is going to make it right.

There are certain things in life that can only be
achieved by you turning to Jesus. Looking unto Jesus
is where you will find all the answers and solutions
to your problems. When you look unto Jesus, you
focus on what He says and what He is going to do
for you. You understand and know where all of your
help comes from, which is God.

The word **looking** is defined as several different
meanings in the Greek or New Testament of the
Bible; however, in Hebrews 12:2, the word **looking**
literally means *to turn (look) away from one thing to*

see another. It comes from the Greek word *aphorao*, which means *to lock into.*

> *"And Peter answered him and said, Lord, if it be thou, bid me come unto thee on the water. And he said, Come. And when Peter was come down out of the ship, he walked on the water, to go to Jesus. But when he saw the wind boisterous, he was afraid; and beginning to sink, he cried, saying, Lord, save me. And immediately Jesus stretched forth his hand, and caught him, and said unto him, O thou of little faith, wherefore didst thou doubt?" (Matthew 14:28-31)*

This looking (locking into) is what allowed Peter to walk on water, when all natural laws stated that it is impossible for a human to walk on water. Peter turned his mental attention away from the boisterous waves and roaring sea and set his regards on or locked into what Jesus said to him, which was to come.

As long as Peter stayed locked into what Jesus said and kept his mind, which is Peter's will and emotions on Christ, Peter overcame his unbelief by walking on water. However, when he turned his attention off Jesus (the Word) and began to pay more attention to what he saw (waves rising) and heard (wind roaring), Peter immediately began to sink.

Every time we turn our attention from God, we will fail. However, as long as we set our will to believe in God, no matter what, God will always allow us to succeed. **There is no failure in God.** His spirit will guide you; therefore, there is no failure in you. Failure only occurs when we get away from God and the things of God.

Looking unto Jesus means that you are gazing, you are setting your attention and focus on what He (Christ Jesus) can do through you. You will stop looking at the past failure, hurts, and disappointments and you will zero in on what God's word has to say about you. Your success in life will only come through Jesus.

You can do what you set your mind to do with the help of God (Mark 9:23). That is right... you can do it! You can break the bad emotion, kick the negative thinking, and be free of the hurt, bondage and sickness. However, for you to overcome these issues, you will need to not let anyone or anything stop you from receiving your blessing.

The words **focus** and **concentration** are synonymous, in that *you will have to zero in on* your challenges. You will have to get a *clear image* of what it is that you need to do and work at getting it done. When a person becomes focused, he or she has his/her mindset on a particular thing. This person focuses on that thing until the desired result is completed.

The word focus is similar to a jet fighter plane; which, when fixed (locked) on the enemies aircraft, it patiently waits until all indicators are a go to launch the missiles. When all indicators are a go and the missiles are launched, the missiles will hit exactly what they are programmed to destroy.

When you fix your mindset on Jesus, negative emotions are destroyed. If you are going to over-come weaknesses, failures and shortcomings, you will need to commit first to Jesus, literally locking into the Word of God, fixing your undivided atten-tion on Him to direct and guide your life.

Notice this scripture, *"I will lift up mine eyes unto the hills, from whence **cometh** my help. My help cometh from the LORD" (Psalms 121:1-2).* What the psalmist says is that his eyes were fixed on God and what He can do for the psalmist. This fixing allowed the psalmist to focus on the positive side of things and not the negative. If things are going to get better, you must believe that they can get better, and with the help of God, they will get better.

> *"A certain woman, which had an issue of blood twelve years, And had suffered many things of many physicians, and had spent all that she had, and was nothing bettered, but rather grew worse, When she had heard*

Jesus, came in the press behind, and touched his garment. For she said, If I may touch but his clothes, I shall be whole. And straightway the fountain of her blood was dried up; and she felt in her body that she was healed of that plague." (Mark 5:25-29)

The woman with the issue of blood stayed focused. She worked through the crowds and did not allow what she went through to stop her from obtaining her promise. With a concentrated focus and an intense effort that was so strong until it could not be denied, she received what she believed.

This woman could have saved herself time, energy and money if she would have looked (turned) her attention to Jesus first. Some people can mean well but never do you any good. This is what the doctors did to this woman, they did her no good, and she went financially broke seeking medical attention. This is not to discredit doctors, because we need them.

The woman with the issue of blood looked to God to understand what He (God) had to say about her condition. God can do what natural law and medical science cannot do. He can heal, deliver and restore at any moment. This woman believed in God's healing power. She fixed her attention on Jesus (the Word of God) and she received healing.

I believe that God can empower his people with good health, especially when you choose to both read the Word of God and pray constantly. *"Dear friend, I pray that you may enjoy good health and that all may go well with you, even as your soul is getting along well" (3 John 2, NIV).* When you choose to physically exercise your body and eat healthy, you will prolong your life, and your mind will prosper.

God will create an environment to where no germs, sickness or disease can be exposed to your body. If any life-threatening illness comes into direct contact with your body, it will die instantly because of the protection that God has placed upon your life.

Why Some People Do Not Change

1.) **Inability to control emotions**—Often, when people are under extreme attack, they will allow their feelings to run wild; they will over-react to situations, and later learn that what they were experiencing was not very bad.

2.) **Sight is not clear**—People who struggle with negative emotions sometimes see things that are not really happening to them. Their vision is off and many times they make bad decisions because they cannot see clearly. They are very skeptical, experiencing thoughts of paranoia and thinking that people are talking about them or out to get them, when the people are not.

3.) Defensiveness—When you protect and shield yourself from constructive criticism and view it as personal attacks, you open up yourself to become defensive. People who tend to shield themselves have little concern about what others think because they are self-absorbed.

4.) Think you know it all—When you think that nobody or only certain people can teach you, you are limiting yourself. You know people who have good information that can be beneficial for you, but these people cannot help you because you think you know it all. You must be open and understand that you can learn from anybody, including a tree, if God is trying to get a message to you.

5.) Pointing the Finger—You cannot recover or overcome negative emotions when you blame others for your problems; in all actuality, you need to point the finger where it belongs at yourself.

How To Manage Your Emotions

1.) **Recognize what makes you hot.** It is important for you to know what sets a fire to your emotions. Is it when people yell or threaten you that make you want to come out fighting like a tiger? Identify what causes you to get wired up and lose control.

2.) **Find a Gym.** Exercise has always been one of the healthiest ways to deal with your negative emotions. Exercise will help you relieve tension and in the same process help to keep your body healthy. Exercise has been proven to make people feel good about themselves.

3.) **Believe that you can change.** There is in every individual an ability to overcome. You can change. It is important not to beat yourself up if you are not changing as fast as you would like. Just keep in mind that it is possible to change and be committed to changing.

4.) **Don't make excuses for inappropriate behavior.** When you respond in a wrong manner, it is important for you to admit that your behavior was inappropriate and unacceptable. When you don't make excuses, you say to yourself that you have to change because what you are doing is not right.

5.) **Think about the long-term consequences of your negative emotions.** When people can look down the road and comprehend how losing their temper on a job would get them terminated and possibly not having any finances for a very long time. This method helps people to slow down on how they will respond to negative emotions.

6.) **Choose the right place and time to express your emotions.** The right place and time will create an atmosphere where you can be relaxed and feel safe to communicate how you feel. This will help you not to feel disrespected in front of others which can trigger old behavior.

Chapter 4

Don't Let Anger Get the Best of You

When you are angry, you really hurt yourself. People will not help you. My wife and I visited a patient in the hospital who was recuperating from an illness for a few days. We were asked by the patient's family to give this patient a visit since the hospital was near our home.

As we were traveling to the hospital, the Spirit of the Lord told me to go by the bank and get some money to bless this patient. When my wife and I walked into the room, immediately we were unwelcome; the patient who knew us very well was very rude and disrespectful.

The patient who knew my wife extremely well was saying things to my wife that I just did not like. Therefore, after listening approximately five to ten minutes of this person's anger toward us, my wife and I agreed to leave. While going home, I remembered that I forgot to give the person the money that I received from the bank.

I allowed the person's anger to throw me off track. That is precisely what anger will do; it will throw you off track. I did not want to upset the patient; therefore, in a hurry to get out of the room, I forgot to give the patient the money which was intended for her. Anger, if misappropriated, will cause hypertension, and distractions; it will throw you off from your intended purpose.

God told me that when people get angry, their blessing passes them by. I wanted to be a blessing to this patient but could not because the patient was mentally hurting too badly to receive it. This patient was so angry, hurt and torn by what she was going through, that the patient's anger caused her not to be helped. Do not run God and people off when you are hurting; be humble and kind to people and they will help you.

When you are rude and ugly with people, you will run people off. The Bible says, *Make no friendship with an angry man; And with a furious man thou shalt not go: Lest thou learn his ways, And get a snare to thy soul" (Proverbs 22:24-25).* Again, this person was so disrespectful; it wasn't until I had left the hospital that I remembered about the money God told me to give. Anger improperly managed causes destruction and confusion. God is not the author of confusion, but peace (I Corinthians 14:33).

Pointers to Controlling Anger

1.) **Change Your Environment**—Try hanging around people who are calm. When you begin to associate with calm people on a consistent basis, you will learn their ways on how to be calm. Also, pull away from those things that infuriate and make you feel trapped. People become angry when they are doing things they don't like to do; find out what you like to do and do it.

2.) **Change how you think**—Angry people have a tendency to be very critical and negative. Very often do they see or say anything good. Try replacing those critical and negative thoughts with words that are encouraging and inspi-rational. Start reading material that focuses only on building you up. Share with others those positive things that you have learned from your readings.

3.) **Schedule your time appropriately**—People often get overwhelmed when they take on more than they can handle. Try scheduling your time to where you are not always in a hurry. When you are constantly in a hurry, you forget things and become upset when people appear to be slowing you down. Manage your time more wisely: If you have a problem with traffic jams, try leaving early or take another route to get to where you need to be comfortably.

4.) **Express Yourself**—There is nothing wrong with you expressing yourself in an assertive, not aggressive or demanding way. Expressing yourself appropriately is healthy because you get what is in you, out. Therefore, you keep yourself from exploding or mild episodes of anger. When you express yourself, you are preventing pressure from building up in you and giving your anger a way of escape so that you will not blow up.

5.) **Choose music and movies that are not aggressive and violent.** Research indicates that when people watch violent movies and listen to aggressive music it tends to stir angry and hostile feelings, thoughts and even make one's blood pressure to arise. Listening to calm music will keep you relaxed and you will not make impulsive decisions.

Chapter 5

What's on Your Mind

For though we walk in the flesh, we do not war after the flesh: (For the weapons of our warfare are not carnal, but mighty through God to the pulling down of strong holds;) Casting down imaginations, and every high thing that exalteth itself against the knowledge of God, and bringing into captivity every thought to the obedience of Christ. (II Corinthians 10:3-5)

Many people are unsuccessful at controlling their emotions because their mind is not healed of past hurts or disappointments. The Bible indicates that the way you get healed of past hurts and disappointments is that you cast down those imaginations and things that try to bring you into captivity.

People who deal with emotional wounds must

be willing to identify where they are in life and are willing to come against those things that do not line up with the Bible. When a person does this they are pulling down strong holds in their mind.

Past hurts and disappointments, if not brought into captivity to the Word of God, will produce shame, guilt, and a sense of low self-esteem. People who experienced victimization in their past often operate in negative emotions. These negative emotions stem from past hurt and abuse that have went unchecked by the Word of God.

You control your emotions by controlling your thoughts, the Bible states, *"Let the wicked forsake his way, and the unrighteous man his thoughts: and let him return unto the LORD, and he will have mercy upon him; and to our God, for he will abundantly pardon" (Isaiah 55:7).* When you forsake negative emotions you are pulling down thoughts that are attempting to lead you in destruction.

The way you control your emotions is not to entertain the negative thoughts but to forsake them, cast them down, replace them with good thoughts by speaking the Word of God over your life. You overcome negative thoughts by replacing them with God's Word. It is God's Word that is going to produce the manifestation of good things to happen in your life.

Notice this Scripture,

> *"Finally, brethren, whatsoever things are true, whatsoever things are honest, whatsoever things are just, whatsoever things are pure, whatsoever things are lovely, whatsoever things are of good report; if there be any virtue, and if there be any praise, think on these things." (Philippians 4:8)*

When you think on things that are true, honest, just, pure, lovely and of good report, you will have those things that you are thinking about. Notice this scripture, *"For as he thinketh in his heart, so is he." (Proverbs 23:7.)* In other words, according to the person's way of thinking, or thought process, it will determine what will be in the person's life.

You are what you think about, what you think about the most is what you will eventually do, and what you do is what you will have. When Adam and Eve thought about eating the fruit in the Garden of Eden (Genesis 3:1-7), their thought process developed into an intense overwhelming or overpowering craving, a feeling or emotion that became so strong until they acted on what they thought about.

Although God had previously instructed them that the fruit was not good for them and was not to be touched. Adam and Eve allowed their negative emotions to overpower them. Although they knew it was wrong, they still did what was wrong because they allowed their negative emotions to control them.

On the contrary to Adam and Eve, when Jesus Christ was tempted by this same tempter in the wilderness (Matthew 4:1-11), Jesus overcame by controlling his emotions. Although Jesus had been fasting forty days and nights and he was very hungry; He did not turn the stones into the bread nor did he do anything that the Devil asked him to do.

Jesus was able to put restrains on what He should not do because He knew that His negative emotions would move him away from God, the same way Adam and Eve's negative emotions moved them away from God.

Again, one of the ways to control negative emotions is to keep your mind on the Word of God and not the negativity you are presently experiencing. The Bible states, *"IF YE then be risen with Christ, seek those things which are above, where Christ sitteth on the right hand of God. Set your affection on things above, not on things on the earth." (Colossians 3:1-2.)* When you set your affection you are looking to God's Word (Bible), you are keeping your mindset focused on the promises of God that are located in the Bible.

Observe the Amplified translation of Colossians 3:1-2,

IF THEN you have been raised with Christ [to a new life, thus sharing His resurrection from the dead], aim at and seek the [rich, eternal treasures} that are above, where Christ is, seated at the right hand of God. [Ps. 110:1.] And set your minds and keep them set on what is above (the higher things), not on the things that are on the earth. (Colossians 3:1-2, Amplified)

Setting your affections is to stay in tune with positive or inspirational thoughts. You will have to keep your mindset deliberately and consistently on God and His Words (the Bible). You will have to confess or say what you believe until the manifestation shows up. You will have to mediate on scriptures concerning what you need and stay on those scriptures until your breakthrough is manifested in your life.

Chapter 6

Speak the Word

Most people ignore **speaking scripture over what they are going through.** The Bible indicates that you will have what you say (Mark 11:23-24). There is another scripture that indicates, *"Let the redeemed of the LORD say so, whom he hath redeemed from the hand of the enemy." (Psalms 107:2)* In the wilderness, (Luke 4:1-13) every time the devil pressured Jesus with temptation, Jesus would verbalize the Word of God and win.

One of the ways to overcome negative emotions is to verbalize the Word of God (Bible) when you are under intense pressure. You do not have to speak loudly; you can speak very softly where no one can hear you, but you must speak the Word. Jesus spoke to Satan and He told Satan what to do, "Get away from me." Satan left Jesus for a season.

"And when the devil had ended all the temptation,

he departed from him for a season" (Luke 4:13). This **season** that the Bible refers to is *a period of time,* which means that negative things will go but they have a way of resurfacing. When they do, you will have to speak the Word of God in order not to fall into temptation.

Notice this scripture, *"And they overcame him by the Blood of the Lamb and by the word of their testimony; and they loved not their lives unto the death" (Revelations 12:11).* If you want your negative emotions or uncontrolled feelings to leave you, then you will have to speak the Word of God over your negative emotions and uncontrolled feelings and tell them to go:

> *"Speaking to yourselves in psalms and hymns and spiritual songs, singing and making melody in your heart to the Lord." (Ephesians 5:19)*

Speaking the Word of God over yourself or someone else, does not mean that your are crazy; in the same way you say a blessing over your food, is the same way you speak a blessing about your situation. You speak the Word of God over life and believe that God's Word is the key that is going to make whatever you need happen.

I find it to be very interesting that when people are

in severe, unexpected sudden danger, they welcome the calling on God. They will say things like, *"O Lord save me! Jesus, help! O my God, Lord have mercy!"* Other people have a tendency to say bad things such as using the name of the Lord God in vain.

The point I am attempting to make is this—if you can speak a Word during unexpected danger, why not speak the Word of faith to make you feel better, to make you motivated about overcoming negative emotions. It is always better to speak in faith than to speak in doubt (Mark 11:23-24).

When King David was dealing with depression, he talked to himself. He said, *"Why am I so depressed? Why this turmoil within me? Put your hope in God, for I will still praise Him, my Savior and my God." (Psalms 42:5, HCSB).* There is nothing wrong with you saying unto yourself that you are a good person, that God loves you, and that you are more than a conqueror. You would be better off saying that than saying all kinds of nasty and evil things about yourself.

Another key thing in controlling your negative emotions is that you must find an appropriate scripture to stand on. Notice this scripture, *"And Jesus answering said unto them, Do ye not therefore err, because ye know not the scriptures, neither the power of God." (Mark 12:24.)* The reason that it is important to find an appropriate scripture to stand on is because you will be zeroing in on the specific nature of your situation. It is the appropriate scriptures that are going to uphold you in times of trouble (Isaiah 41:10).

Chapter 7

Esau Madness

*A*nd Jacob sod pottage: and Esau came from
the field, and he was faint: And Esau said
to Jacob, Feed me, I pray thee, with that
same red pottage: for I am faint: therefore
was his name called Edom. And Jacob said,
Sell me this day thy birthright. And Esau
said, Behold, I am at the point to die: and
what profit shall this birthright do to me?
And Jacob said, Swear to me this day; and
he sware unto him: and he sold his birthright
unto Jacob. Then Jacob gave Esau bread and
pottage of lentils; and he did eat and drink,
and rose up, and went his way: thus Esau
despised his birthright. (Genesis 25:29-34)

In examining the life of Esau's madness, let us take
a look at the word faint. Most people will define the

word **faint** as *to cave in, give up or quit*. I would like to examine a different side of this word faint. The word **faint** in its original language is to become *weary* or *weak*. It carries with it the connation of *letting go or releasing what you have.*

This is what Adam and Eve did in the Garden of Eden. They released the authority (dominion) that God gave them over to the devil because they became weak over a fruit (Genesis 3:1-24). The interesting thing about the Garden of Eden temptation is that Satan did not take anything; Adam and Eve released their authority (dominion) over to him when they became emotionally weak.

When a person is weary or weak during times of temptations, or if the person has not gained some sense of control or restraint during pressured times, they will give in or release the things that they value most. When you release something, you turn it over. A good example of this is the story of Esau's birthright.

Again, one day Jacob cooked a pot of stew. Esau, his brother, came in from hunting and was extremely hungry. Esau asked for some stew but his brother refused to give him any unless Esau sold (*released*) his birthright to Jacob. Esau released his birthright signifying that he cared very little for it.

A **birthright** is *an inheritance*—which all the

children had a right to share (Luke 15:11-13)—however the portion of the firstborn child's was to be two times bigger than all the other children's inheritance. If there were three children, the inheritance would be divided in four parts. The firstborn child was to receive two parts, and the remaining two children were to receive one part each (Deuteronomy 21:17).

The point I want to make about Esau is that when he released his birthright this started an avalanche of psychotic behaviors that drove Esau to the point of almost losing his mind. Esau actually thought that Jacob deceived him into selling his birthright, but realistically, Esau chose to release it.

Notice this scripture,

"Esau replied, "My brother deserves the name Jacob because he has already cheated me twice. The first time he cheated me was out of my right as the first-born son, and now he has cheated me out of my blessing." Then Esau asked his father, "Don't you still have any blessing left for me?" (Genesis 27:36, CEV)

Esau eventually became so mad and angry with his brother Jacob that he wanted to kill him (Genesis 27:41). Esau felt that Jacob had cheated him twice, but actually, Jacob had only cheated him once, which was out of his father's blessing. For whatever reason, Esau failed to deal with the fact that he sold his birthright to Jacob for a pot of stew.

Esau was the responsible party, not Jacob. When Esau sold his birthright, it was no longer stolen because he had turned it over to Jacob. Esau released to Jacob all of the blessings that would be associated with the first-born inheritance.

Apparently, Esau never let the anger go of selling his birthright because later he accuses Jacob of stealing. Again, this lie indicates addictive behavior on Esau's part because he never owns up to his own responsibilities. In addition, if Esau had admitted giving Jacob his birthright, things would have been better inside Esau.

In a nutshell, all of Esau's problems evolved out of the fact that he became too relaxed; he released his blessing to his brother. Therefore, because Esau could not handle the fact that he released his blessings, he got mad, resulting in him wanting to faint, to just cave in, give-up and quit.

I have experienced people who appear to be very successful for a long period, then all of a sudden, they hit bottom. Everything appears to fall apart or go wrong in their lives. I believe that these people became too loose and relaxed; they felt that because they had arrived to success, they did not have to do anything to keep their success.

Notice this scripture: *"Therefore we ought to give the more earnest heed to the things which we have heard, lest at any time we should let them slip" (Hebrews 2:1).* When you start letting things slip and slide by, that is when you set yourself up for a fall.

The disappointments of life often occur when you become too relaxed. How can an individual know when he/she is slipping? You are slipping when you no longer value the Word of God above everything that you say and do.

When you faint, you become stagnant; you lose your grip on your focus and start slipping. In boxing terms, you drop your guard. You become too tired or relaxed, which can result in the possibility of a knock out.

The Bible tells us,

"Be well balanced (temperance, sober of mind), be vigilant and cautious at all times; for that enemy of yours, the devil, roams around like a lion roaring [in fierce hunger], seeking someone to seize upon and devour."
(I Peter 5:8, AMP)

When you faint, you relax until you do not do

anything, which opens the door for whatever you are struggling with to come on you and overpower (*seizing or devouring*) you to the point of you shutting down, making you have no desire to continue.

The way to overcome when you feel like giving up is to keep doing what you know to do (John 8:31-32). You have to stay with it; you cannot allow negative emotions, immediate discomfort, or dissatisfaction to cause you to lose heart and quit. Sometimes in life you will just have to ride things out; you just have to stick with it and enjoy the ride (Hebrew 10:35), making the best out of a not-so good situation.

Chapter 8

Enduring the Storms of Life

I remember a time when I was traveling home from the seminary in Cleveland, Tennessee. Right before I came to the North Carolina state line it began to rain very hard. The rain was consistent and would not let up. I knew that I had an appointment to make and I needed to get there. Therefore, I slowed down, turned on my headlights and flashers and continued to move forward very slowly. Within less than five minutes, I was out of the storm.

Now let us diagnose the storm situation. Life struggles are the same way: **First,** we decide that we are going to make it (Matthew 9:29). Although the storm was bad, I slowed down because it was not bad enough for me to stop. That is important, because your situation cannot get so bad that God cannot get you through it. I think I need to say that one more time...your situation cannot get so bad that God cannot get you through it.

The important thing to note here is that you have to keep on moving forward. You cannot allow negative opinions and difficult situations to cause you to stop, turn, or derail you from what God wants to do in you.

One of the main things that will get you through the storms of life is that you will keep on moving forward. Although you might not have it all together, and things might even appear not to be working for you, know that God is with you. He will lead you safely through the storms of life.

Second, in regards to life struggles, you have to learn how to make adjustment. What I mean by adjustment is doing something different that will ultimately make you come out ahead. Adjustment does not mean that it did not work, but you have to do something different in order to obtain the results you are looking for. That's awesome. Rather than calling your attempts that came up short, failures, why not call them opportunities for advancement.

I often watch college football, and in one particular game, the quarterback was having challenges that day. The game was about mid-way into finishing; the quarterback had thrown three interceptions and had fumbled one time.

The announcer of the game kept saying, *"They must get the quarterback out; they have to get him out of there if they're going to have a good chance at winning this game."* Well sure enough, the coach pulled the quarterback out of there, and the team came back and won the game, all because they made the necessary adjustments.

My point is this—in life just because things are not working that well at the moment does not mean you throw in the towel and quit; maybe you need to do like the announcer said about the quarterback— switch it up or do something different. Many times when things are not working, it is because we have not made the necessary adjustment to get it right; therefore I encourage you to get it right.

Often, people do not achieve or receive because they do not believe in God or themselves. **You can do it** is based on the fact that you will believe in God and yourself no matter what. *"And Jesus said, [You say to me], If You can do anything? [Why,] all things can be (are possible) to him who believes!" (Mark 9:23, NLT.)* It does not matter what you hear, see, know, or even feel. God is able to do the great and awesome thing in your life, if you will only believe Him.

The **third** thing I did in this storm was that I stayed the course; I did not turn back. I did not even pull over to the side of the road. I slowed down and proceeded with care and safely went through. Just because things happen in your life that you do not like, you cannot allow those things to get you off course. You must stay the course because you can do it. You cannot quit, because on the other side of the storm the sun is shining and there is a brighter day.

The songwriter says,

"Though the storm keeps on raging in my life, and sometimes its hard to tell the night from the day, Still that hope that lies within is reassured as I keep my eyes upon the distant shore. I know He'll lead me safely to that blessed place He has prepared, but if the storm doesn't cease and if the wind keeps on blowing, my soul has been anchored in the Lord"

I would like to point out two additional keys to getting through the storms of life. **First**, the storm does not have to keep on raging in your life. You can do something about it. **Second,** you must take authority over the storm and tell it what to do. Therefore, if you do nothing then nothing is going to happen; you must demonstrate action to obtain the things that you desire.

"And there arose a great storm of wind, and the waves beat into the ship, so that it was now full. And he was in the hinder part of the ship, asleep on a pillow; and they awoke him, said unto him, Master, carest thou not that we perish? And he arose, and rebuked the wind, and said unto the sea, Peace, be still. And the wind ceased, and there was a great calm." (Mark 4:37-39)

Jesus took action over what was opposing them (the storm); He woke up and did something about the situation. If you do not appreciate the results that you are getting in life then do something about that dissatisfaction. Jesus encouraged his disciples not to be afraid; if they would take action just as He (Jesus) did, they would have had the results that they desired.

The Bible says in Luke 10:19 *"Behold, I give you power to tread on serpents and scorpions, and over all the power of the enemy: and nothing shall by any means hurt you."* The storms of life can cease by you speaking and acting on what you know to do. That is right—you can speak to the storm or the mountain, and you can tell it to be still or be at peace; what you say will happen, according to Mark 11:23-24.

> *"Yea, though I walk through the valley of the
> shadow of death, I will fear no evil; for thou
> are with me; thy rod and thy staff they com-
> fort me." (Psalms 23:4)*

There are two things to note about this verse: 1) You will only go through for a certain period of time; you will come out when you go through. You are only going through temporarily and not permanently. You do not pitch a tent and settle down in your challenges. When you go through, your eyes should be firmly locked to where you are going and not what you are going through. Struggle is the indicator that you have not stopped moving.

2) You do not have to fear what you are going through because God is with you, and because God is with you no weapon formed against you shall prosper (Isaiah 54:17). Fear is the enemy of faith. Where fear is present, faith is absent. When you know that God is with you, He will protect, guide, comfort and deliver (Psalms 138:7). God will give you the strength to make it through.

The Bible says,

> *"AND JESUS being full of the HOLY GHOST
> returned from Jordan, and was led by the
> Spirit into the wilderness, Being forty days*

> *tempted of the devil. And in those days he*
> *did eat nothing: and when they were ended,*
> *he afterward hungered." (Luke 4:1-2)*

The only thing the devil could do to Jesus was tempt him. The word **tempted** in Luke 4:2 is *peirazo* which is pronounced *pi-rad'-zo;* it means to *test, try* or *prove*. It is important to say,

> *"Blessed is the man who perseveres under*
> *trial, because when he has stood the test,*
> *he will receive the crown of life that God*
> *has promised to those who love him. When*
> *tempted, no one should say, "God is tempt-*
> *ing me." For God cannot be tempted by evil,*
> *nor does he tempt anyone; but each one is*
> *tempted when, by his own evil desire, he*
> *is dragged away and enticed. Then after*
> *desire has conceived, it gives birth to sin;*
> *and sin, when it is full-grown, gives birth*
> *to death." (James 1:12-15, NIV)*

According to scripture, God does not tempt anyone; however, the devil is very different. His purpose is to examine and challenge your faith in God, to destroy every potential promise of you becoming great in God.

The devil plans to get people addicted to drugs,

alcohol, cigarettes, perversion, unlawful sexual activities, overeating, lying, killing, cheating, anything that is evil or causes death. (John 10:10) The devil's plan is to get you tangled up in despair until you believe that there is no hope to live any longer.

When you yield yourself to certain bad emotions, you become the slave to them; in other words, the thing you surrender yourself to is the thing that will be responsible for bringing you down or lifting you up.

Scripture says, *"Know ye not, that to whom ye yield yourselves servants to obey, his servant ye are to whom ye obey; whether of sin unto death, or of obedience unto righteousness?" (Roman 6:16)* The thing to note about you yielding yourself to negative emotions is that the sole cause for the catastrophe in your life is you.

This is vital to know because you cannot blame the devil or people, although the devil or evil spirits do work through people, nevertheless, evil spirits or people cannot make you do anything (Psalms 91:10-11).

You have to be aware of how people can be used; people are used by the devil to get you into bondages, addictions, and bad habits. Some people may be smart, good-looking, and even intelligent, but if Satan is behind their actions, He will ultimately destroy them and you.

Temptation begins in the mind (II Corinthians 10:3-6). This is why you need to guard what you see, hear and think, because those things can have negative effects upon what you do. The thing about negative emotions is that they will try to trigger or stimulate you to do the things you see, hear and feel, although you know that it is not right for you to be doing those things. Just because things look, sound, or feel good does not mean that they are right, especially when they contradict the Word of God.

It is also important to note that the devil had no power or control over Jesus' life. Jesus was able to overcome every negative emotion; every manipulative tactic, and every trickery maneuver of the devil. (Luke 4:3-13) Therefore, you can overcome; you can overcome every negative desire and bad emotion that attempts to take you away from the will of God for your life.

You do not have to hit bottom, you do not have to lose everything; God has designed you to be a winner; God has designed you to bounce back, to get up and to go to your victory.

Notice this scripture: *"The Lord shall increase you more and more, you and your children" (Psalms 115:14).* The word **increase** means to *add up,* it means *(enlargement, escalation, multiplication, to heighten or widen, and to expand.)* That is what God desires to do in your life; He wants to increase you with good. The Bible says that you are more than a conqueror (Romans 8:37). No weapon formed against you shall prosper, (Isaiah 54:17) and nothing by any means shall hurt or harm you (Luke 10:19).

In the Garden of Gethsemane (Matthew 26:51-53), Jesus was not tempted to fight during his arrest, but Peter was tempted to fight and this was clearly demonstrated by Peter cutting off the soldier's ear. Immediately, Jesus restored the soldier's ear because Jesus is love, restoration, forgiveness and healing.

During the time of Jesus' arrest, He spent quality time in prayer. The reason Peter was confused and angry was because he spent very little time in prayer. Peter was sleeping when he should have been praying.

The Benefits of Prayer

1) **King Hezekiah,** The prophet Isaiah came to him and informed him to get his house in order because he was going to die of his sickness. King Hezekiah immediately prayed to God and God heard the King and added 15 more years to his life; if the King would have not prayed, he would have not lived 15 extra years (II Kings 20:1-6).

2) **Jonah** was physically going down to Hell and called on God. God heard him and delivered him. The prophet's life was spared from death because he prayed to God. (Jonah 2:1-10)

3) **Peter** was released from prison because prayer was made fervently and consistently by the Church. (Acts 12:5-16) When you pray, it will enable God to get involved to release you from everything that is attempting to keep you in prison or locked down.

Chapter 9

Adam and Eve's Uncontrolled Emotion

"*N*OW THE serpent was more subtle than any beast of the field which the LORD God had made. And he said unto the woman, Yea hath God said, Ye shall not eat of every tree of the garden? And the woman said unto the serpent, We may eat of the fruit of the trees of the garden: But of the fruit of the tree which is in the midst of the garden, God hath said, Ye shall not eat of it, neither shall ye touch it, lest ye die. And the serpent said unto the woman, Ye shall not surely die: For God doth know that in the day ye eat thereof, then your eyes shall be opened, and ye shall be as gods, knowing good and evil. And when the woman saw that the tree was good for food, and that it was pleasant to the eyes, and a tree to be desired to make one* *wise, she took of the fruit thereof, and did eat, and gave also unto her husband with her; and he did eat. And the eyes of them both were opened, and they knew that they were naked; and they sewed fig leaves together, and made themselves aprons. And they heard the voice of the LORD God walking in the garden in the cool of the day: and Adam and his wife hid themselves from the presence of the Lord God amongst the trees of the garden. And the LORD God called unto Adam, and said unto him, Where are thou? And he said, I heard thy voice in the garden, and I was afraid, because I was naked; and I hid myself... So he drove out the man; and he placed at the east of the garden of Eden Cherubims, and a flaming sword which turned every way, to keep the way of the tree of life." (Genesis 3:1-10, 24)*

There are some things that can be learned as a result of Adam and Eve being emotionally ruled in the Garden of Eden. **First, indulging in the wrong thing will make you act the wrong way.** If you eat too much, you will get sick. If you worry too much, you will get depressed. When people get under the influence of wrong behaviors, they do and say things that they would never do or say if they were not under the influence of wrong behavior.

Notice that Adam and Eve hid themselves because they saw that they were naked. Their uncontrolled emotions lead them to gratify their flesh; caused them to respond in a way that was unnatural; they saw things that God did not want them to see. That is what an unrestrained spirit will do to you; it will cause you to act and do things that are unhealthy or unnatural for you, ultimately destroying your life if you do not regain control of your emotions.

Second, do not make impulsive decisions. Many times people get into trouble when they make impulsive decisions, especially when they do not know the persons or the product that is luring them. It is extremely important to talk with someone about the major decisions you make.

Notice this scripture: *"Where no counsel is, the people fall: But in the multitude of counselors there is safety" (Proverbs 11:14).* Adam and Eve fell into sin because they did not bounce their decision off God as to whether or not to eat the fruit. If they would have checked it out with God first, they could have avoided eviction from the Garden of Eden and the consequences of eating the forbidden fruit.

It is important to note that the devil came to Eve

asking her questions about what God said, making it appear that God was not telling the truth and that God was withholding something good from them. The same manipulative approach that the devil used with Adam and Eve is being used in today's society.

People from all types of occupations try to promote and sell their products. If you do not know what you need, you can buy things or get involved in things that will cause you to suffer and experience great loss, taking you away from the will of God for your life.

Before you make any decision that is in opposition to the information that you know to be true, you should not buy or commit to anything. Let people know that you will get back with them after you have prayed about the situation.

If you seemed pressured at that point to make an immediate decision, then that's not God. Do not make any decisions under the influence of pressure. I have seen sales people pressure people into purchasing things that they do not need and the purchaser struggle to keep the merchandise that was purchased—if not lose it.

People who come into your life will either help you or set you back. Wrong association will keep you addicted and bound to what you need to be set free. In other words, it is important for you to be **self-differentiated,** not taking on others' advice when you know exactly what you need to do. When people tell you to do things contrary to what's right, when you are self-differentiated, you can say no, stepping away, feeling no sense of guilt or responsibility to anyone.

Third, it is important to check out your association with people. *"And we beseech you, brethren, to know them which labour among you... " (I Thessalonians 5:12).* When you know people because of association, you are aware of what they are capable of doing and what they are not capable of doing.

Before Adam and Eve made any decisions about the fruit they ate, they should have sought God about the devil's credibility. They should have done a background check on the devil; this would have provided them with accurate information to determine if what the devil was saying was true.

Here are **four biblical references** regarding the importance of association: (1) Lot was blessed because of his association with his uncle Abraham. (Genesis 13:5-6) (2) The mariners were cursed because of their association with Jonah. (Jonah 1:12) (3) Laban acknowledged that he was blessed because of Jacob. (Genesis 30:27) (4) The nation of Israel was cursed because of their association with

Achan. (Joshua 7:1-26)

> *"And everyone that was in distress and everyone that was in debt, and every one that was discontented, gathered themselves unto him; and he became a captain over them: and there were with him about four hundred men." (I Samuel 22:2)*

One of the ways to get the blessings of God upon your life is to get connected with blessed people. King David was blessed by God; people knew this by gathering themselves unto him. The people knew that King David had a yoke-destroying and burden-removing anointing.

The anointing that was in King David's life spilled over into their lives. This is what you call **increase by association**. The same way you can increase by right association, you can decrease by wrong association.

The definition for the word **bless** is an *empowerment to prosper;* it is a way of God enabling you to produce effective results. It is an ability to get the job done and to get the job done right. The definition for the word **curse** is an *empowerment to fail;* it is an inability to produce effective results. The curse is associated with Satan and its result is always failure.

If you do not want the curse, you will have to disconnect from cursed people and cursed things. Therefore, your association with people will do two things; either it will bless you or curse you.

Chapter 10

Learn the Vocabulary of Silence

"*To everything there is a season, and a time for every matter or purpose under heaven… a time to keep silent and a time to speak.*"
(Ecclesiastes 3:1, 7)

According to this particular passage of scripture, there is a time and a season for everything. That means that there is a time to deal with complicated issues and a time to leave them alone. There is a time to voice your concern and a time to leave them alone. To everything, there is a time and a season.

An example of understanding the vocabulary of silence is when I was called and asked to help serve at a **home going celebration.** A home going is not a funeral; the word funeral has the association of sadness, hurt and grief. When a believer goes home to be with the Lord you should be excited for them; they are in a better place, a place of no more pain, sorrow, hurt or inabilities, therefore, there is nothing to be sad, hurt or in grief about (Revelation 14:13, 21:1-5).

However, the family needs to be both comforted and supported during this time. In addition, the family needs to implement some techniques and approaches to deal with the separation or detachment of no longer being physically able to be present with their loved one.

I was asked by one of the leaders of the home going ministry to have all the volunteers for the service to arrive one hour before the service started. On the day of the home going, I spent a good amount of time that morning in prayer. I was uncertain if I was going to attend because of my work schedule. Nevertheless, I felt the prompting of the Holy Spirit to go and serve during the home going.

Upon walking through the door and getting in my position to serve, immediately one of the volunteers of the home going ministry walked up to me and began to let me have it. This person was loud and was very disrespectful to me. This person was upset because I had asked this person to arrive one hour before the service started to set up and to make sure everything was in place.

I told the person that I was instructed by the authority over me to have everyone arrive at that particular time. This person refused to hear any of that, and said that I was to tell the exact time of the home going so they could arrive when the home going would start. In addition, this person told me other things that I chose not to write.

Because this person was unreasonable and intolerant, I became silent and walked away, mainly because I was tired of being disrespected in public. There were many people walking around us that day.

During the home going service, I noticed that some of the family and friends were walking in and out. I went out of the service to comfort a young man. After talking with this man for about five minutes, he accepted Jesus Christ as Lord and Savior outside of the building. He became born-again before he returned to the service.

I observed another young man walking out of the service. This man told me that he was present when his friend died. He saw and heard things that he felt no one else could understand but him, because he was with the person when they breathed their last. This brother also accepted Jesus Christ as Lord and Savior of his life, and returned to the service saved, born-again, forgiven, healed, and restored.

The point I am making in saying this: At the beginning of the home going service a volunteer member was very disrespectful and embarrassing to me. This person's attitude included derogatory words and they did not feel or sound good, but I kept my mouth shut.

I refused to become a victim of those negative words that were spoken to me. I used the vocabulary of silence to control my emotions. I knew that if I could just walk away and not argue, but pray in the Holy Ghost to myself, I would be keeping myself in the love of God (Jude 1:20-21). This would keep me sensitive to the move of God to be a blessing to the people of God.

The key to successfully using the vocabulary of silence is to keep you from saying the wrong words and to keep your mind on God. Scripture tells us to set our affection on things that are above (Colossians 3:1-2). Setting your affection on things that are above is mentally and spiritually establishing what you say and do to be uplifting, which can be done by you understanding the importance of your words.

Many people talk themselves out of the blessings of God. They speak negatively or they are amassed in negative activities that distract them from the presence and blessings of God. Distractions cause them to lose focus of God's intended purpose. During the home going service I stayed focused, and God was able to show His strength through me (II Chronicles 16:9) to help two young men turn their lives over to Him (Jesus Christ).

These two young men became born-again because I controlled my tongue; I exercised the vocabulary of silence. If I would have argued with the disgruntled volunteer, or would have become angry or shut down, I would not have experienced the blessing of God using me.

The Message Bible says, *"I am determined to watch steps and tongue so they won't land me in trouble. I decided to hold my tongue as long as Wicked is in the room" (Psalms 39:1, TM).* There are times when you hear negative things (wicked), you will need not to respond, but just keep your mouth shut and pray softly to yourself.

Again, God could not have used me if I would have been caught up in a spirit of anger, bitterness, or unforgiving attitude with this volunteer member. *"Let no corrupt communication proceed out of your mouth, but that which is good for the use of edifying, that it may minister grace into the hearers" (Ephesians 4:29).* Often, when people get mistreated they get mad and their tongues are like loose cannons. If you cannot say something good about a person, it is better to not say anything at all.

> *"Wherefore, my beloved brethren, let every man be swift to hear, slow to speak, slow to wrath." (James 1:19)*

Some people need to learn the art of just keeping their mouths shut; they then would receive deliverance and breakthroughs. It is the mouth that often gets people in trouble. Therefore, silence is an art that the Body of Christ definitely needs to master.

The Bird and the Frog

There is a story about a bird and a frog. They both needed to go south for the winter. The frog came up with an idea as to how the bird could possibly get him there. The frog suggested to the bird, "If you would allow me to grab your legs with my mouth, then you can flap your wings and the both of us could fly south for the winter."

The bird thought about that statement in amazement, wondering how the frog came up with such a good idea. The bird shook his head in agreement and said, "Okay. I can do that." The frog grabbed the bird's legs with his mouth and off they flew, flying south to enjoy the heat.

As they were flying south, a farmer was working in the field. He noticed the bird was flying and how the frog was holding on to the bird's legs with his mouth; they were both successfully flying south for the winter.

As the bird and the frog continued to fly south, the farmer thought out loud and said; *what an ingenious idea, that is just brilliant! I wonder who could come up with such an ingenious idea*? And about that time the frog opened its mouth and said its mi———ne, its mi———ne and fell right to the ground and splattered.

The moral of the story is this **if you open your mouth at the wrong time, it can cost you.** This is oh so true in controlling your negative emotions, because there are times that you need to keep your mouth shut and just believe God; everybody does not need to know your business. In most cases, the only time some people are aware of your struggles is when you tell them.

Another interesting thing to note about the frog is that the frog forgot the old saying that says, *"Think before you speak."* If the frog could have just only implemented the "think before you speak" technique, the frog would not have died.

There were times when Jesus did not even respond to people (Matthew 27:12). I believe one of the reasons Jesus did not respond to some people's questions is that it was not necessary to respond, and sometimes if you respond to foolish questions, your answer will only complicate the matter.

The Bible says, *"But avoid foolish questions, and genealogies, and contentions, and strivings about the law; for they are unprofitable and vain (Titus 3:9).*

Many people, often, are caught up in the mouth trap; their mouths often get them into situations that they do not want to be in. Therefore, in those situations it is better to just keep quiet.

Think about this for a moment. The only reason a fish is hooked is that it opens its mouth. The fish getting hooked has nothing at all to do with the sophistication, expensive fishing bate or the expertise of the fisherperson.

The fish is hooked solely because the fish opened its mouth. I do not compare anyone to an animal, but Jesus often used animals and nature to better paint the picture of what he was attempting to communicate.

Notice how fish respond when they are caught—they resist, pull back, kick, and flop all over the place. So, what is happening? The fish is in a situation that it does not want to be in; if the fish had to do it all over again, it would definitely keep its mouth shut. Therefore, when you keep your mouth shut, and learn the vocabulary of silence, being silent will keep you from being hooked or caught up in things you do not want.

When most people are going through or experiencing great difficulties, it is very seldom that they say anything good. They are very negative about themselves and very negative about others:

"So the men Moses had sent to explore the land, who returned and made the whole community grumble against him by spreading a bad report about it—these men responsible for spreading the bad report about the land were struck down and died of a plague before the LORD. Of the men who went to explore the land, only Joshua son of Nun and Caleb son of Jephunneh survived." (Numbers 14:36-38, NIV)

God held these negative men's mouths responsible; God took the bad report of these men so seriously that they all died the <u>same day</u> they spoke negative. Only Joshua and Caleb survived because they set a watch over their tongues.

The Bible says, *"Those who love to talk will experience the consequences, for the tongue can kill or nourish life (Proverbs 18:21, NLT).* Your mouth will hold you responsible before God; you will have what you said whether or not you are conscience of it. What you say will grow and develop, thus you become what you say.

God gave humans two of just about everything; He gave them two feet, two legs, two arms, two ears, two eyes, two hands and two holes in the nose, but interestingly, a human's mouth, God gave only one.

Could it be that God in His Omniscience (*all knowing ability*) knew that man would run his mouth twice as much as he would work with his hands and hear with his ears? Scripture indicates for us to be *"slow to speak… " (James 1:19).*

What you say affects how you think, and what you think affects what you do. What you do is what you are going to have. This is why the Bible says,

> *"For verily I say unto you, That whosoever shall say unto this mountain, Be thou removed, and be thou cast into the sea; and shall not doubt in his heart, but shall believe that those things which he saith shall come to pass; he shall have whatsoever he saith."* (Mark 11:23)

You cannot say things like *"I am always messing up,"* because you will always mess up. You have to say what you desire, and not confess the negative stuff you are presently experiencing. If you say, *"I will never recover,"* or *"I will never get out of this,"* then you won't.

If you can consistently speak that you believe that you will receive healing, restoration, freedom and recovery, then that is what you are going to have (Mark 11:23-24). Therefore, you can control your emotions and you can be all the good things that God's Word says that you can be. (Deuteronomy 28:1-14) Congratulations on how to control your emotions.

About the Author

Loy B. Sweezy, Jr is a graduate of East Coast Bible College in Charlotte, North Carolina, with a Bachelor of Science Degree. While at East Coast Bible College, he did missionary work in India, Germany and Jamaica. He is a graduate of the Church of God Theological Seminary in Cleveland, Tennessee, with a Master's Degree.

After receiving his Master's Degree, he moved back to Charlotte, North Carolina, where he worked as a Chaplain in pastoral care and counseling for Carolina Medical Center. Later he moved to Birmingham, Alabama, to work at Princeton and Montclair Hospital in pastoral care and counseling. There he met a lovely lady named Nyouka D who later became his wife. He is currently working on a doctoral degree at Oral Roberts University in Tulsa, Oklahoma.

Contact Information

To contact the author write:
  Loy Sweezy Ministries
  P.O. Box 131
  Austell, Georgia 30168

You can order this book and other materials
by calling toll-free 1-866-873-6330

Internet Address: www.loysweezy.com

Please provide your personal testimony or how this
book has helped you when you write. Your prayer
requests are welcomed.

Books by Loy B. Sweezy, Jr

- *Breaking Free*
- *Overcoming Bad Habits*
- *How to get out of a Tough Spot*
- *Let Go or Get Dragged*

Notes

Notes

www.ingramcontent.com/pod-product-compliance
Lightning Source LLC
Chambersburg PA
CBHW021343290326
41933CB00037B/543